THE GREAT OUTDOORS! ➡

Hiking
and
Backpacking

MC

Mason Crest

THE GREAT OUTDOORS!

Camping

Discovering Nature

Fishing

Hiking and Backpacking

Horseback Riding

Hunting

Mountain Biking

Snow Sports

Survival Skills

Water Sports

THE GREAT OUTDOORS!

Hiking
and
Backpacking

JOHN McKINNEY

Mason Crest
450 Parkway Drive, Suite D
Broomall, PA 19008
www.masoncrest.com

Printed and bound in the United States of America.

Series ISBN: 978-1-4222-3565-2
Hardback ISBN: 978-1-4222-3569-0
EBook ISBN: 978-1-4222-8314-1

First printing
1 3 5 7 9 8 6 4 2

Produced by Shoreline Publishing Group LLC
Santa Barbara, California
Editorial Director: James Buckley Jr.
Designer: Patty Kelley
www.shorelinepublishing.com

Cover photographs by Dreamstime.com/Galyna Andrusko.

Names: McKinney, John, 1952- author.
Title: Hiking and backpacking / by John McKinney.
Description: Broomall, PA : Mason Crest, 2017. Series: The great outdoors
   Includes webography and index.
Identifiers: LCCN 2016002438| ISBN 9781422235690 (Hardback) | ISBN
   9781422235652 (Series) | ISBN 9781422283141 (EBook)
Subjects: LCSH: Backpacking--Juvenile literature. | Hiking--Juvenile
   literature.
Classification: LCC GV199.6 .M425 2017 | DDC 796.51--dc23
LC record available at http://lccn.loc.gov/2016002438

CONTENTS

Chapter 1: Take a Hike! 6

Chapter 2: Hiking the Right Way. 16

Chapter 3: Choosing the Right Gear 26

Chapter 4: Further Adventures 36

Find Out More. 46

Series Glossary of Key Terms 47

Index/Author 48

KEY ICONS TO LOOK FOR

Words to Understand: These words with their easy-to-understand definitions will increase the reader's understanding of the text, while building vocabulary skills.

Sidebars: This boxed material within the main text allows readers to build knowledge, gain insights, explore possibilities, and broaden their perspectives by weaving together additional information to provide realistic and holistic perspectives.

Research Projects: Readers are pointed toward areas of further inquiry connected to each chapter. Suggestions are provided for projects that encourage deeper research and analysis.

Text-Dependent Questions: These questions send the reader back to the text for more careful attention to the evidence presented here.

Series Glossary of Key Terms: This back-of-the-book glossary contains terminology used throughout this series. Words found here increase the reader's ability to read and comprehend higher-level books and articles in this field.

Educational Videos: Readers can view videos by scanning our QR codes, providing them with additional educational content to supplement the text. Examples include news coverage, moments in history, speeches, iconic sports moments and much more!

calories a measurement of energy burned by a body

loop trail a hiking path that begins and ends at the same point

trailhead the point at which a hiking path begins

CHAPTER 1

Take a Hike!

magine a **loop trail** that takes you and your friends through a forest to the top of a hill. It returns along a stream. In your day pack you have all the right gear and best trail mix ever (because you made it yourself).

At first your group travels through the forest. The birds are singing and it's easy hiking. Then the trail climbs above the trees and gets very steep. Goodbye shade, hello hot slopes. You zip off the legs of your pants and turn them into hiking shorts. It's hard walking uphill, even though you're on a well-built trail.

One of your friends is new to hiking and is having trouble keeping up. You stop for a drink of water, give her some trail mix (with chocolate!) and tell her, "You can do it!" You put her in the front of the line and all of sudden she turns into a rocket ship and blasts up the hill! Before you know it, you've all reached the top.

What a view! Mountains and more mountains. And lots of blue sky.

Then you hike down the mountain to a meadow where a deer leaps across the trail. As the deer looks back at you, you act quickly and take some great pictures of the deer standing in some wildflowers.

Near a stream you reach a trail junction without a sign. You know to take a left and hike downstream back to the **trailhead**. But after a few minutes you realize you're not going in the direction of the waterfall. You check the map. Oops—should have gone right back there instead of left.

You double back and soon reach the waterfall, which isn't very big, but big enough to fill a waist-high pool. Time for a quick dip to cool off!

As you head downhill to finish your hike, you remember the great pictures you took . . . of your friend new to hiking looking sad and then happy . . . of splashing in the water, and everyone standing proudly on the top of the mountain.

Those pictures—and your memories—will be great to share with family and friends until you start planning your next hiking adventure!

Well-marked trails point the way.

Amazing vistas await hikers who head into the backcountry or the hills.

Super Popular

hat's the most popular form of outdoor recreation in North America?

No, it's not swimming or soccer or bike riding.

It's hiking. And most adults who enjoy time on the trail got started as kids or teens.

Hiking is taking a walk on a trail in nature. Walking to school on sidewalks is not hiking, and neither is walking around the mall. But walking a path in the forest or a trail in the mountains is hiking. So is walking a path in the desert or along the seashore. Every hike is a walk, but not every walk is a hike.

Hiking takes you to beautiful places you can only reach on foot. Trails lead to waterfalls, meadows full of wildflowers, mountaintops, swimming holes, picnic areas and campgrounds.

Taking a walk in the woods with friends makes the walking much easier!

The dictionary definition of a hiker is a simple one.

hiker: *one who hikes (especially frequently); a foot traveler; someone who goes on an extended walk in the mountains or country (for pleasure)*

In other words, a hiker is one who likes to walk in nature just for fun!

Lots of young people like to hike. They hike with their friends, their families, the Girl Scouts, the Boy Scouts, and other groups. They hike with their teachers and classmates and with rangers and guides in nearby nature parks.

About one in every five people in the U.S. and Canada go hiking every year. Hiking is also very popular in Europe. Chances are if you like walking in nature and getting away from it all, you're a hiker. You just haven't thought of yourself that way.

You don't need to travel far away to go hiking. You might discover wonderful hiking trails in parks and nature preserves close to home.

A hike can be as short as a half-hour or a half-day, or many days long. Some people hike the same trails near home over and over again. Others explore new trails in faraway mountains.

Physical Benefits of Hiking

Backpacking is a combination of hiking and camping. A backpacker hikes into the backcountry to spend one or more nights there, and carries supplies and gear for preparing meals and sleeping. A backpacker can travel farther into wilderness areas away from people and cities than a day hiker can. Many backpacking trips take place over a weekend while others are a week or many weeks in length.

Hiking is one of the simplest outdoor activities that people can take part in. It is also one of the most rewarding. It's a great way to spend time with your friends and family. It feels good to be out in the fresh air, get some exercise and enjoy the wonders of nature.

Not everybody sees the joy in hiking, though. To some people, hiking means being too hot or too cold, blisters and mosquito bites, and fears about snakes, bears and getting lost. Some people think hiking is just too hard and nature too scary, and they want no part of the challenges that come with being in the great outdoors.

For sure hiking, like all outdoors sports, has its challenges.

Adding elevation to your hike increases the physical benefits.

HIKERS DICTIONARY

Hikers have their very own vocabulary. Here are a few "hiker words" to get started.

Backpack *(noun)* A large pack worn on the back to carry camping gear; *(verb)* to go on an overnight hike carrying your gear in a backpack.

Day hike A hike that begins and ends during daylight hours.

Day pack Small, soft backpack made especially for hikers.

Degree of difficulty Measurement of how hard the hike is; ratings include easy, moderate, and difficult.

Elevation Measurement of altitude above sea level; the difficulty of a hike goes along with how much elevation gain is required.

Fleece A soft, lightweight fabric.

Junction The point at which a trail meets another trail.

Layering Wearing several thin layers of outdoor clothing rather than one heavy one.

Nature The world of living things and the outdoors.

Nature trail A path with signs identifying plants and describing other natural features.

Pace The speed at which you hike.

Summit The top of a mountain.

Switchback A zigzag, back-and-forth route up a mountain.

"Take a hike!" "Leave!" or "Go away!" But for hikers—taking a hike is a good thing!

Terrain The natural features of the land.

Zip-off pants Pants that can be unzipped to become shorts.

But overcoming those challenges—steep trails, difficult weather conditions, feeling like you can't take another step—to complete your hike is very satisfying. Even if a hike gets very difficult at times, you'll feel proud of yourself once you've accomplished what you set out to do.

Hiking is known as "a lifetime sport"—a fun outdoor activity you can do your whole life. Hiking has many benefits: it makes the heart stronger, improves balance, and increases endurance. Hiking can lead to a happier, healthier, and often longer life.

Hiking has many of the same benefits as walking and running, and some special ones, too. Because every step a hiker takes along a trail is a little bit different (uphill, downhill, over rocks), hiking gives muscles a special kind of workout.

Hiking really burns off the **calories**. Someone weighing 100 pounds (45 kg) burns off 360 calories per hour while hiking hills and 285 calories per hour hiking flat trails. (Swimming uses 275 calories per hour, riding a bike uses 250 calories per hour.)

Hiking with a pack increases the calories burned; so does hiking faster and going uphill. By comparison, sitting around watching TV or play-

Burn calories, get fit, and create memories when you strap on a backpack.

ing video games burns only about 50 calories an hour. There's no question that hiking is a lot better for you than gaming and many people say it's a lot more fun, too.

Exercise . . .
and calm: Benefits of
the outdoors.

A lot of young people feel rushed and over-scheduled (with more organized activities and homework than their parents had), under pressure to get good grades, and spend way more time than they'd like riding around in a bus or car. And then there are those typical teen concerns about fitting in and figuring it all out.

Mental Benefits, Too

 hike in nature can help you relax. In recent years, a whole lot of research has suggested that hiking helps students get more focused and helps put people of all ages in a better mood. Some hikers think it's pretty funny that scientists are finally "proving" that hiking is good for you!

So what is there to learn about hiking? You just put one foot in front of the other, right? It's so simple.

Well, not that simple. And actually there's more to hiking than just walking.

This book shares the basics of hiking so that you can better enjoy this fun way to spend time outdoors. You'll learn easy ways to select hiking gear you really need, how to choose a hike that's right for you, how to trav-

The solitude and quiet of nature on a hike can provide lasting and relaxing benefits.

el safely and have a great time in nature. Plus you'll get some great tips on how to make the most of your time on the trail.

You don't have to be super-fit to be a hiker. You can choose a hike that's right for you, and have a great time in the great outdoors. Nature might be closer than you think, and you can learn about it—just by hiking through it.

This book will help you think, then act like a hiker; you'll become a hiker by actually hiking. We learn by doing, whether that's snowboarding, playing the guitar, or hiking.

So let's gear-up and get ready to take a hike. And consider telling your friends, parents and teachers to "Take a hike!", too.

In a nice way, of course.

TEXT DEPENDENT QUESTIONS

1. What is the word for the beginning of a trail?
2. Name a physical benefit of hiking.
3. Name a mental benefit of hiking.

RESEARCH PROJECT

Find three different trails in your area. Look at maps of each and write a short report about it. Describe the length, the direction, the type of terrain covered, and what people might see on the way.

CHAPTER 2

Getting It Done Right

good hiking trail is like a good guide, pointing things out and picking the very best route from place to place. The best hiking trails don't go from point A to Point B in a straight line or in the fastest way, but take the scenic route. A good trail **switchbacks** (zig-zags) up and down a mountainside rather than heading straight up.

Trails lead to beautiful spots in nature, to places to

📖 WORDS TO UNDERSTAND

duck (cairn) a pile of rocks near a trail used to mark the route

hydration pack a pack that hold water and lets you drink from a tube

multi-use trail a trail that permits more than one user group at a time (hiker, horseback rider, mountain biker, etc.)

pace the speed at which you hike

switchback a zigzag, back-and-forth route up a mountain

17

BUCKEYE TRAIL
↑ JAITE 4 M.
BLUE HEN FALLS→

Be sure to follow posted trail signs that provide distance and direction.

view wildlife, to the tops of mountains, to meadows full of wildflowers, to historic sites, to rivers and lakes, to campgrounds and picnic areas.

The first trail-makers were wild animals, breaking down brush as they traveled to and from water. Native Americans used animal trails and made new ones. Miners and loggers also made trails.

More than a hundred years ago, people began building trails, lots of them, just for hiking. Trails don't just happen; they're designed and built. What a hiker sees on a trail is often created by a trail designer.

Most hikers don't think about who keeps trails repaired, but in most cases it's the trail users themselves who do the work. Consider volunteering to work on a trail where you like to hike. It's hard work digging and clearing brush but it feels really good knowing that you're keeping the trails open and doing something for your fellow hikers.

Choosing a Trail

hat's a great trail? It's a question as difficult to answer as "What is great art?" For some hikers, it's a wilderness trail far from the city. Other hikers like trails in the forest, the desert, or in the hills near home.

Trails and hikes are rated by their level of difficulty—usually easy, moderate, or difficult. For example, an easy hike might be less than 5 miles (8 km) with an elevation gain of less than 700 feet (215 m) or so. A moderate hike might be 5 to 10 miles (8 to 16 km) with less than a 2,000-foot (610-m) elevation gain. A difficult hike might be more than 10 miles long with an elevation gain of more than 2,000 feet.

Hikers can choose among many different kinds of trails. Nature trails are short trails that help you learn about plants and the nearby environment. An out-and-back trail is one you use both coming and going. Many hikers like loop trails because you circle around and see something different with every step along the way . . . and you end up where you began.

Often the best trails are hikers-only paths (no other users permitted) and single-track (wide enough for only one person) trails. **Multi-use trails** permit more than one group at a time (horseback riders, mountain bikers, hikers).

PACING YOURSELF

- Choose the pace that's best for you.

- Rest once an hour for five to ten minutes. To keep your momentum and to avoid stiffness, several shorter rest periods are better than one long one.

- Set a steady pace, one you can keep up all day.

- Wear a watch, not because you have an appointment with a waterfall and need to be on time, but because a watch gives you an idea of your pace and helps you get back to the trailhead by dark.

On the Trail

t's important to know how fast you hike (your **pace**) so you can choose a trail that's a good length for you. Find a pace that you can keep up for a long time. You need to know your limits, but you should also challenge yourself.

Adults hike 2 to 3 miles (3.2 to 4.8 km) an hour. Kids hike about 1 to 2 miles (1.6 to 3.2 km) an hour. Your speed will vary depending on the difficulty of the trail. Adults are often surprised how far kids can go in one day and kids surprise themselves, too.

Pick a hike to have the right distance, elevation, and weather for your family.

Hiking speed is very different for each person. Here are three speeds for comparison:

- *Hiking on level or near-level ground*   *2 to 3.5 mph (3.2 to 4.6 km)*
- *Hiking uphill or at elevation*   *1.5 to 2 mph (2.4 to 3.2 km)*
- *Very steep climbs*   *0.5 to 1.5 mph (0.8 to 2.4 km)*

Be weather-wise. Dress for whatever weather you're hiking in—and expect it to change. Know where you're hiking. Get a basic idea of where you started the hike and where you're going. Learn how to read a map and keep oriented.

Work as a team. Offer comfort to your friends or younger family members if they're slow, tired or don't feel well. Use kindness and encourage them with positive words. Help them out by carrying some of their things in your pack, or by offering water or a little snack. Think about how you would want to be treated if you felt the same way—and then do it.

There's no whining in hiking. You know how awful it is to be around someone who whines. If you feel like whining, do something else instead! Have a snack, drink some water, slow down, speed up, take a look at the view, pretend you're an animal...anything, but don't whine.

Hikers choose their gear based on the weather they will face.

Hiking is fun, but there are some important safety tips. First, always stay with your fellow hikers. Second, to keep from getting lost (and to protect the environment), stay on the trail. Pay attention to signs, mileage markers, posts, and piles of stones known as **cairns** or **ducks**.

Notice the landmarks you pass, such as unusual trees or rock formations. Stop now and then to compare your progress to the route on the map.

Another way to stay on course is to look behind you once in a while.

See what the land looks like from the other direction. Knowing where you came from always gives you a better feel for where you're going and prepares you for the return trip.

Always think for yourself. Even if you're in the middle or at the end of a line of hikers, pay attention to where you're going.

Trail Maps

hen you're hiking in an unfamiliar place, you need a map that shows the trails. You can go online, download a map and print it out, use a park or trails app on your phone, or pick up a paper map at a park or ranger station. Some park maps are very simple and show only the trails themselves, roads, and some features such as the visitor center and picnic areas. More detailed hiking maps show trailheads, creeks and rivers, elevations, and distances between points.

Key to reading a map is the scale, which shows how many inches represent a mile. If one inch equals one mile on a paper map, and it's about three inches from the trailhead to your destination, you're looking at a three-mile hike.

Also check the map's legend, which tells you what the symbols on the map mean. The symbol for a campground might be a tent; for a ranger station, a little cabin with a flag on top.

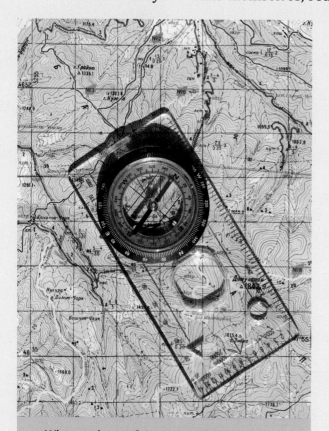

Who needs apps? A topographic map and a compass are the "old-fashioned" way.

Modern GPS devices, apps, and online maps can provide great information.

Fun On and Off the Trail

ust being out in nature with your friends can be fun, but some things make a good hike great—like water. Swim, splash, or just cool your feet in a lake or stream.

For some hikers, the best thing about being out in nature is seeing animals and interesting plants and trees. Ask park rangers to point out places where you're likely to spot wildlife while you're on your hike. You can also try to spot evidence of animals, such as footprints, scratches on tree bark, nests, hair, and more.

The plants you see can inspire ideas, too. See how many different types of flowers you can spot on your hike, or how many types of trees you find. Are there any you've never seen before?

Hikers who conquer the top of hills might find that other hills await them.

Depending on where you live, you might also be able to look for signs of early people. Did Native Americans or First Nations people live in your area? Evidence of their long-ago lives might still be seen. Some trails even take you to places where you can see cave paintings or former settlement sites.

Maybe you'll get summit fever, which sounds like something that makes you sick, but is actually a good thing for a hiker to catch: it means that you must hike to the top of the mountain and nothing will stop you. Some hikers feel so good about reaching a mountaintop and signing the summit register (often a notebook in a can), they decide to become "peak-baggers" and hike to the top of many more mountains. Peak-baggers "collect" peaks (all the peaks higher than 3,000 feet (915 m) in a mountain range, for example) and keep records of their climbs.

Another fun thing to do is to take pictures of your hike to share back home and online. Start with pictures of the trailhead or trail signs and then take pictures of your smiling buddies as they hike along the trail. Get close-ups of faces. Get close-ups on nature, too: one big flower close-up is usually a better image than a lot of flowers in a faraway meadow.

TEXT DEPENDENT QUESTIONS

1. What's considered an easy hike? A difficult one?

2. How could you encourage a friend who is having a hard time hiking uphill?

3. What are some of ways you can be sure to stay on the trail and avoid getting lost?

RESEARCH PROJECT

Research a trail you'd like to hike. Explain where the trail goes, interesting features along the way, and how long and how difficult a hike it is.

CHAPTER 3

Get Great Gear!

ood gear—hiking clothing and accessories—makes an important contribution to a hiker's well-being and safety. While good gear alone doesn't mean you'll for sure have a good hiking experience, it certainly can help!

Good hiking gear—particularly clothing—can be expensive, but it sure doesn't have to be. A hiker doesn't have to spend like a skier or a golfer to have a good time on the trail.

To get started hiking, you don't need a whole lot of high-tech equipment. The basics are a day pack, good hiking boots, and outdoors clothing.

WORDS TO UNDERSTAND

headlamp a light source worn on the head for hiking and camping in the dark.

layering adding layers of clothing to stay warm and removing layers to cool off.

Choosing a Good Day Pack

day pack is a soft pack that attaches to your shoulders and usually includes a hip band or waist belt for support. It is okay to begin hiking with a school backpack (as long as you don't bring your books and homework, ha!), but if you want to be a real hiker, you need a day pack made to carry the things a hiker needs: the Ten Essentials, extra clothing, food, water.

Padding is very important to a comfortable day pack. Packs come in many models and sizes so try on several packs to find out which one is the best for you. Some hikers prefer hydration packs, which carry lots of water that you can sip from a tube while you're hiking.

Features of a good day pack
- Durable weather-proof fabric
- Padded shoulder straps
- Padded back
- Wide, padded belt
- Plenty of pockets and compartments
- Side pouch for water bottle
- Strong buckles and straps
- Covered zippers
- Strong grab handle

When packing a day pack, remember:

1) Pack stuff you'll most likely use on the hike in the places easiest to reach

2) Pack the heaviest items at the bottom of the pack, the lightest ones toward the top.

Hiking boots are lightweight but sturdy, often covering the ankle for extra support.

Hiking Boots

The best choice is a pair of the lightweight version of hiking boots that are more like sneakers with a heavier sole. Make sure they fit your feet with plenty of toe room for downhill hiking, and are wide enough for comfort. If the boots are a good fit, you'll start out and stay blister-free.

Many hikers can wear new, lightweight hiking boots straight out of the box and onto the trail. If they feel a little stiff, though, break them in before you hit the trail.

Socks made especially for hiking prevent blisters, stay drier and are much better than cotton ones. Take an extra pair. If you get your feet wet, you'll be happy to have dry socks to wear.

THE TEN ESSENTIALS

What must you always take on a hike? A Ten Essentials list was first shared among hikers in the 1930s and is still used today.

1. **Map:** One that shows all the trails.

2. **Compass:** Goes hand-in-hand with the map. Bring a GPS unit, too.

3. **Water:** Bring plenty and drink before you're thirsty.

4. **Extra Food:** Bring more than you think you might eat. Your hunger or day's plans might surprise you, and you'll want to be prepared.

5. **Extra Clothes:** Pack rainwear and be ready for sudden changes in weather.

6. **First Aid Kit:** Be sure to bring blister-treatment stuff, too.

7. **Pocket knife**: Very handy. Keep it clean and sharp.

8. **Sun Protection:** Sunglasses and sunscreen.

9. **Headlamp/Flashlight:** You never know when you might have to hike after dark.

10. **Matches and Firestarter:** Waterproof matches and something to get the flames going if you have to light an emergency fire.

Along with the Ten Essentials, consider packing these items:

- **Insect Repellent:** Keep those bugs away!

- **Trekking poles** give you third and fourth "legs" on the trail.

- **Bandana,** to soak in water and wrap around neck to keep your cool on trail.

Clothing

This video lays out the essentials of safe and positive hiking.

The best way to pick clothing for a hike is to understand what hikers call **layering**. Layering is just what it sounds like: you add layers of clothing when you're cold and remove layers of clothing when you get warm. If it's cold, rather than wearing one heavy sweater, wear two or three thinner layers. That way, if you get warm, you can remove any or all of the layers of clothing.

Hiking clothes made of synthetic materials will keep you dry as you start to work harder and sweat more. The best materials are soft, lightweight, and moisture wicking. Here's a good layering plan:

T-shirt Begin with a synthetic (not cotton) T-shirt. There are many colors and styles to choose from!

Long-sleeved shirt Next add a synthetic (not cotton) long-sleeved shirt.

Fleece jacket Looks great and keeps you warm. It doesn't weigh much so that when you take it off and stuff it in your pack, it's easy to carry.

Rain jacket/Windbreaker Keep a lightweight one in your pack. It will likely come in handy when you least expect it.

Long pants are best in cold weather and some hikers like them in warm weather, too, because they protect against scratches and sunburn. Many hikers like to wear zip-off

Rain gear can always be taken off and stowed if the weather clears up.

pants. These are long pants with zippers above the knee so you can zip off the bottom half, changing them into shorts.

Hats keep body heat in, solar heat out. A hat protects you from heat and cold because your body actually heats up and cools off through your head. A baseball cap is fine, and a hiker hat with a big brim is even better.

Food

t's okay to pack a basic lunch with a sandwich, fruit, and a cookie. Experienced hikers like to pack a variety of healthy and high-powered trail foods that can be eaten throughout the day. Here are some of our favorite trail foods

Dried fruit Easy to pack, won't spoil, very tasty.

Jerky Plenty of protein and a cave man experience: the chance to gnaw away at dried meat in the middle of the wilderness.

Cheese and crackers Hard cheeses pack much better than soft.

Ants on a log Fill celery stalks with peanut butter and raisins.

TRAIL MIX

GORP, which stands for "Good Old Raisins and Peanuts," and also called trail mix, have been a part of hiking for a long time. But if trail mix only had raisins and peanuts it wouldn't be nearly as popular as it is. Hikers have added all kinds of stuff to it over the years and everyone has their own favorite mix.

Making your own trail mix at home is easy and fun and allows you to throw together foods and flavors you really love: granola, M&Ms, carob chips, dried fruit (cranberries, apple, apricot, peach, mango, pineapple), banana chips, flaked coconut, shelled sunflower seeds, soy nuts, almonds, cashews.

Stopping for an energizing snack is a great
time to check the map and your directions.

Bars Energy bars, granola bars, protein bars, sports bars, whatever
you want to call them. Keep a few in your pack. If you don't eat them
that day, they can keep for the next hike.

Chocolate Tastes great at home, even better on the trail.

Water and Cooking

inally, get a quality, heavy-duty water bottle, with a loop-
top design so you'll never lose the lid. Be sure to take—and
drink!—plenty of water while you're hiking. As ridiculous as it
sounds, many hikers who remember to pack water don't take the time
to drink it.

"Drink before you're thirsty" is the hiker's rule. Bring your entire
water supply for the day so that you'd don't have to drink from streams
and lakes, which may not have pure water and could make you sick.

Some advanced hikers carry small filters that can remove nearly all
of the unsafe material from water found in nature. Some filters can at-
tach to the top of a water bottle. If you choose these to add to your water supply, read the instructions carefully to make sure you understand

what the filter can and can't do.

Backpackers take the Ten Essentials and all the gear carried by day hikers, plus a tent, sleeping bag and cookware. Carrying your bedroom and kitchen on your back can mean a heavy pack. Backpacker's Law #1: If you want it with you, you have to carry it! Backpackers are crazy about getting the most lightweight gear: a 4-pound tent is way better than an 8-pound tent!

Backpackers use small liquid-fuel camp stoves and boil water to add to special backpacking food called freeze-dried food. Some of these in-

At the end of a hike, a safely-built campfire is perfect for marshmallows!

stant meals are yummy and some yucky, so taste test before your take them on the trail! Of course nothing tastes too bad when you're really hungry and camping in a beautiful place.

Don't expect restrooms, hot showers and a camp store when you backpack into a trail camp. A hike-in camp might have a table and a fire ring. Some trail camps are just small patches of level ground.

The best way to learn about backpacking is to go on an overnight hike with an experienced backpacker.

 TEXT DEPENDENT QUESTIONS

1. What are some of the features of a good day pack for hiking?

2. Explain how a hiker uses "layering" to dress for all kinds of weather.

3. What must a backpacker take to camp overnight?

RESEARCH PROJECT

Choose a pair of boots you'd like and explain why they'd be a good choice for you and the kind of hiking you do.

Watch and learn:
How to pack a backpack
for hiking

CHAPTER 4

Further Adventures

ow long is "hiking season"? For some hikers, who live where temperatures are mild, hiking season is all year. Other hikers enjoy three seasons of hiking—spring, summer and fall—and only have to put their hiking boots in the closet in the winter.

Part of being a hiker is being prepared for all kinds of weather. Wherever—and whenever—you hike, you need to take precautions in hot and cold weather, and on rainy days.

WORDS TO UNDERSTAND

National Parks the greatest nature and historic parks in the U.S., under the care of the National Park Service.

National Scenic Trail America's most beautiful long (over 100 miles in length) trails.

Triple Crown Trails Appalachian Trail, Pacific Crest Trail, and Continental Divide Trail.

Finding a Hike near Home

Some people think hiking is only a weekend activity and you have to make a long drive far into the mountains to find a trail. Not true! Often you can find a place to hike near your home. Look for trails in city, county and state parks, greenways and neighborhood pathways. Often there are paths to hike along nearby streams, ponds and lakes.

You might be surprised what a little research might find in the way of parks and trails. Here's what to look for:

A walk in the park Parks in the city and in the suburbs often have lots of trails

Make tracks Many thousands of miles of out-of-use railroad tracks

A head covering is vital in the hot, dry conditions of a desert hike.

have been changed into walking paths. Check out www.railstotrails.org to find a trail near you.

Walk with the animals Nearby wildlife preserves, marshes and bird-watching sites often have trails leading to them.

Go to college There's often a fitness trail, garden or nature path on campus.

Take the bus Sometimes you can ride the bus right to a trailhead.

Hot Weather Hiking Tips

 ecent studies have shown that the best temperature for hiking is 50 F to 55 F. Above this range, a hiker's performance goes down. As temperatures rise, hikers must adjust.

- Time your hike for the cool of the day. Early morning is best, late evening second best. Avoid mid-day when the sun is directly overhead.
- Wear a hat
- Apply sunblock (minimum SPF 15) on all exposed skin.
- Wear loose fitting, light-colored lightweight clothing
- Carry—and drink—lots of water.

Cold Weather Hiking Tips

 et all the synthetic-fabric clothing you have and get ready to do some serious layering. Wear heavy socks and weatherproof boots

- Get the latest weather report and adjust your trip with regard to any storms approaching.
- Pack waterproof outer layers of clothing.
- Wear a hat, scarf or hood, gloves or mittens.
- Drink plenty of fluids
- Eat regularly, with lots of high-energy snacks
- Use trekking poles to keep balance on slippery slopes

Rainy Day Hiking Tips

I f you hike enough, sooner or later, you'll hike in the rain. Some hikers would rather be rained on than be rained out and cancel their hike. Hiking in the rain can be an OK—even fun—experience, if you stay dry.

- Carry Rainwear. Experienced hikers aren't surprised by sudden wet conditions.
- Unzip your pits. Assuming your rain gear has armpit zippers, regulate your temperatures by zipping and unzipping your pit zips.
- Keep stuff dry. Use self-sealing plastic bags to keep your map, food, and clothes dry.
- Enough is enough. It's fine to hike in the rain up to a point. If you get wet and cold, though, get back to the trailhead and hike again another day.

Make sure you bring snacks and water for your dog if he joins you!

Many dogs love to hike. If your four-legged friend is in good condition and dogs are allowed where you're hiking, bring your dog along. "Indoor" dogs or out-of-shape "couch potato" dogs might have a hard time on the trail and it might not be wise to take them hiking.

If you do bring the dog, remember to:

- Make sure your dog has current identification tags.
- Bring water and a collapsible bowl. Dogs get thirsty and overheated just like humans.
- Obey leash laws.
- Don't allow your dog to chase squirrels, deer or wildlife.
- Clean up after your dog.

National Park Trails

America's **national parks** are beautiful and have great hiking trails. Some parks are known as "hiker parks" because hikers come from all the way across the country and from all over the world just to take a hike in them. National Parks with terrific trails include Acadia, Bryce Canyon, Zion, Grand Teton, Olympic, Isle Royale, Rocky Mountain, Yellowstone and Yosemite.

In Canada, National and Provincial Park hiking trails include Kejumkujik in Nova Scotia, Galloping Goose in British Columbia, and Grey Owl Trail in Manitoba. Plus, check out Granite Ridge Trail in Ontario and the Lake Louise Tea House Challenge in Alberta.

America's Appalachian Trail stretches for more than 2,000 miles through 14 states.

Long-Distance Trails

America has eleven terrific long-distance trails called National Scenic Trails and more than 1200 great shorter trails known as National Recreation Trails. The two most famous trails are the Appalachian Trail (2,172 miles/4,634 km) that extends across the forests and mountains of the eastern U.S. and the Pacific Crest Trail (2,655 miles/4,272 km) that extends from the desert to the High Sierra to the Cascades; the AT and PCT, as they're known, along with the Continental Divide Trail (3,100 miles/5,000 km) are known as the Triple Crown of long-distance trails.

Other National Scenic Trails include the

No time for a full hike? Here's a short spin along the Appalachian Trail.

Florida NST (1,400 miles/2,253 km), the Potomac Heritage NST (700 miles/1,126 km) and in Wisconsin the Ice Age NST 1,200 miles (1,931 km). Hikers who complete one of these long-distance trails are known as end-to-enders.

Using the information and tips in this book, you can be a safe and happy hiker. There is nothing like discovering the great outdoors one step at a time!

TEXT DEPENDENT QUESTIONS

1. What are some tips for hiking in hot weather?

2. How long is "hiking season" where you live?

3. Where could you find a place to hike near home?

RESEARCH PROJECT

Choose a "hiker park" or a long-distance trail and explain its attractions to someone who likes to hike.

John Muir Trail *(California)* It might be America's most famous trail, 215 miles (346 km) across the mighty High Sierra, from Yosemite National Park to the top of Mt. Whitney (elevation 14,505 feet/4,421 m), which just happened to be the highest point in the continental U.S. Plus granite peaks that touch the sky, lovely lakes and meadows filled with Sierra wildflowers.

John Muir Trail

West Coast Trail *(British Columbia)* A 47-mile (75.6-km) trail along the coast of Vancouver Island that attracts hikers from all over the world. Fabulous beach walks, a hike through a rock arch, forests of ancient trees and magnificent waterfalls.

Columbia River Gorge *(Washington and Oregon)* America's second largest river, rain forests and high waterfalls are highlights for the hiker. The trail features more than 100 waterfalls, including 620-foot (188 m) Multnomah Falls.

Grand Canyon National Park *(Arizona)* Descending into the canyon, hikers encounter some of the most spectacular views available on the planet—a look at two billion years of the earth's history revealed by the Colorado River. It's an awesome hike way down to the bottom of the canyon but remember one important thing: you have to hike back up!

Yellowstone National Park *(Wyoming, Montana)* The huge park has big animals—moose, bear and bison—and trails that lead to weirdly colored pools, geysers that shoot steam to the, high peaks, great forests, and beautiful lakes.

Grand Canyon National Park

Jasper National Park *(Alberta)*, a large park in the Canadian Rockies, gives the hiker a chance to see glaciers, hot springs, lakes and lots of wildlife: elk, moose, bears, beavers, caribou and bighorn sheep.

Great Smoky Mountains National Park *(Tennessee and North Carolina)* is "great" for hikers with 800 miles (1,286 km) of trails leading

Great Smoky Mountains National Park

to thundering waterfalls, clear rivers and spruce fir forests. Outstanding spring wildflowers and fall colors.

Long Trail

Long Trail *(Vermont)* Hike 270 miles (434 km) along the nation's oldest long-distance pathway through the wildest forests and up to the highest peaks of the Green Mountains. Many hikers choose to stay overnight at the many hiker huts located along the trail.

Hawai'i Volcanoes National Park *(Hawai'i)* Crater Rim Trail takes hikers through an active volcano! Hike up the Kalauea and Mauna Loa volcanoes, through lava fields, a desert and a rain forest. 120 miles (193 km) of amazing trails!

Ozark Highlands Trail *(Arkansas)* The 200-mile (321-km) trail leads to lakes, wooded valleys, amazing rock formations, hundreds of creeks and waterfalls. Known for its spring and fall colors.

Volcanoes National Park

FIND OUT MORE

WEBSITES

americanhiking.org
Learn all about hiking and hiking trails from the American Hiking Society.

gorp.com
The Great Outdoor Recreation Page covers advice about how to hike and where to hike.

TheTrailmaster.com
Tips and stories for the hiker; the author's official website!

pc.gc.ca
Hiking information for the National Parks of Canada

nps.gov
The National Park Service provides information here for all the national parks.

BOOKS

McKinney, John. *The Hiker's Way*. Santa Barbara, Calif.: Olympus Press, 2013. The author shares his lifelong love of hiking as well as tips on how hikers can contribute to the "greening" of the world.

Skurka, Andrew. *National Geographic: The Ultimate Hikers' Gear Guide*. Washington, DC: National Geographic, 2013. Hiking successfully means having the right gear; this is the one-stop shopping guide.

Townsend, Chris. *The Backpacker's Handbook, 4th Edition*. Washington, DC: National Geographic, 2013. The massive book won't fit in your backpack, but it will have info to make every trip a success.

SERIES GLOSSARY OF KEY TERMS

bushcraft wilderness skills, named for the remote bush country of Australia

camouflage a pattern or disguise in clothing designed to make it blend in to the surroundings

conservation the act of preserving or protecting, such as an environment or species

ecosystem the habitats of species and the ways that species interact with each other

friction the resistance that happens when two surfaces rub together

insulation protection from something, such as extreme hot or cold

layering adding layers of clothing to stay warm and removing layers to cool off.

rewilding returning to a more natural state

synthetic manmade, often to imitate a natural material

traction the grip or contact that an object has with another surface

wake the waves produced by the movement of a boat

INDEX

benefits 11, 13, 14, 15

boots 29

Canadian parks 41

cold weather tips 39

choosing trail 19, 20, 38, 39

clothing 31

dog, hiking with 41

food 32, 33

gear 27-32

history 18

hot weather tips 39

long-distance trails 42, 43

National Parks 41

packs 28

popularity 9

rain, hiking in 40

speed 21

"Ten Essentials" 30

trail maps 22

trail mix 32

water 34-35

wildlife 23

PHOTO CREDITS

ABOUT THE AUTHOR

John McKinney is the author of 30 books about hiking, parklands and nature, including *The Hiker's Way, Hike Smart*, and *Hike for Health & Fitness*. John, also known as The Trailmaster has hiked and described more than 10,000 miles of trail across America and around the world. A strong advocate for hiking and our need to reconnect with nature, John shares his expertise on radio, TV, online, and as a public speaker. Learn more at TheTrailmaster.com.